AF268643

Writerly PAPERIE

Rainbow Watercolor

STATIONERY PAPER

25 SHEETS | 5.5" x 8.5" | Half-Letter Size Paper | Simply Cut Out & Use

  Simply Cut Out & Use

Simply Cut Out & Use

Simply Cut Out & Use

Simply Cut Out & Use

Simply Cut Out & Use

Simply Cut Out & Use

Simply Cut Out & Use

Simply Cut Out & Use

Simply Cut Out & Use

www.ingramcontent.com/pod-product-compliance
Lightning Source LLC
Chambersburg PA
CBHW042119030726
47599CB00002B/270